DATE DUE

J

DOMESTIC DOGS

COCKER SPANIELS

by Susan H. Gray

The Child's World

Published in the United States of America by The Child's World®
1980 Lookout Drive • Mankato, MN 56003-1705
800-599-READ • www.childsworld.com

Our thanks to Michael Bosch and everyone at the Marin Humane Society and
the Animal Miracle Foundation for their assistance in making this book possible.
In memory of Honey.

PHOTO CREDITS

© Daniel Dempster Photography/Alamy: 25
© DK Limited/Corbis: 29
© iStockphoto.com/Lori Carpenter: 19
© Judith Collins/Alamy: cover, 1
© Marin Humane Society: 17
© Mark Raycroft/Minden Pictures: 9, 13, 27
© Norcia/New York Post/Corbis Sygma: 23
© Peter Beck/Corbis: 15
© Robert Dowling/Corbis: 11
© Tammy McAllister/BigStockPhoto.com: 21

ACKNOWLEDGMENTS

The Child's World®: Mary Berendes, Publishing Director;
Katherine Stevenson, Editor

The Design Lab: Kathleen Petelinsek, Design and Page Production

LIBRARY OF CONGRESS CATALOGING-IN-PUBLICATION DATA

Gray, Susan Heinrichs.
  Cocker spaniels / by Susan H. Gray.
    p. cm. — (Domestic dogs)
  ISBN-13: 978-1-59296-963-0 (library bound : alk. paper)
  1. Cocker spaniels—Juvenile literature. I. Title.
  SF429.C55G73 2008
  636.752'4—dc22   2007020792

Table of Contents

NAME That DOG!

What little dog was named after a bird? ❀ What dog once lived in the White House? ❀ **What dog loves to run an obstacle course?** ❀ What dog needs to have its ears cleaned often? ❀ Did you say the cocker spaniel? ❀ Then you are correct!

5

Spaynels and Spaniels

Over 600 years ago, a writer lived in England. His name was Geoffrey Chaucer (JEFF-ree CHAW-sur). He wrote about a dog called the spaynel. Spaynels were hunting dogs. They loved the outdoors.

There were two main groups of spaynels. Some loved to leap into the water. They fetched birds that hunters had shot. They became known as water spaniels. Others hunted on dry land. They became known as land spaniels.

England is on the island of Great Britain, in Europe. Scotland and Wales are on Great Britain, too. The map below shows where Great Britain is on Earth. The map on the right shows a closer view.

Atlantic Ocean

Scotland

North Sea

Northern Ireland

Ireland

England

Wales

Great Britain

Atlantic Ocean

English Channel

France

7

Many kinds of dogs came from these two types of spaniels. They got their names from the things they did well. Irish water spaniels loved to swim. Springer spaniels surprised birds. They made the birds spring into the air! And cocker spaniels hunted birds called woodcocks. That is how cocker spaniels got their name.

"Cockers" were great hunters. They were also friendly and smart. People saw that they made good pets. The dogs became **popular** in Europe. Soon, people brought them to the United States. The cute little dogs caught on there, too. Today, they are one of America's 20 most popular dog **breeds**.

President Richard Nixon had a cocker spaniel named Checkers. Checkers died in 1964. His grave is in Wantagh, New York.

8

This cocker spaniel looks almost as if she is smiling!

9

Charming, Sturdy Little Dogs

Cocker spaniels are small dogs. They are only about 15 inches (38 centimeters) tall at the shoulder. Adults weigh 20 to 30 pounds (9 to 14 kilograms).

Cockers have friendly faces. Their big brown eyes make them look sweet and thoughtful. Cockers raise and lower their eyebrows. That can make them look puzzled or sad. Cockers' long, soft ears add to their charming look.

Many cockers have this type of haircut. The hair on the back is cut short. The hair on the legs and ears is left longer.

Cocker spaniels have soft, silky hair. Their beautiful coats can grow very long. The hair can be straight or a little wavy. Cockers can be black, brown, red, or cream colored. Some are white with patches of other colors.

These dogs have short legs and deep chests. Even though they are small, they are strong! They like to be outdoors. They love to run and swim.

Cocker spaniels belong to a dog group called sporting dogs. Sporting dogs like to hunt. Golden retrievers and Irish setters are sporting dogs, too.

There are two breeds of cockers—the Cocker Spaniel and the English Cocker Spaniel. English Cocker Spaniels are larger.

Here you can see two types of cocker colors.

13

Great Dogs, Great Pets

There are many reasons why cockers are so popular. These dogs are friendly, gentle, and loving. They are happy and playful. They want to please their owners.

Cockers get along well with children and other pets. This is especially true if they are adopted as puppies. Older dogs can be adopted, too. But they need more time to get used to new people.

This cocker loves to be with her family.

Some cocker spaniels are real barkers. They bark when the doorbell rings. They bark at strangers. They might even bark at much bigger dogs. Gentle training can help them settle down.

Many cocker spaniels like to go for car rides. They like to feel the wind. A car ride made one cocker a hero! Her name was Honey. Honey and her owner were riding in the car. The car tumbled down a steep hill. It landed on its roof. Honey wiggled through an open window. She ran to a neighbor's house. She led the neighbor to the car. Honey's owner was badly hurt. People were able to pull him out. Honey had saved her owner's life!

Cockers do well in small homes. They just need to get out and exercise.

Cocker spaniels should be walked on a leash. As hunting dogs, cockers want to run free. But they can easily run off. They can get lost or hurt.

Here you can see Honey with her owner. She saved his life!

Cocker Spaniel Puppies

Most cocker spaniels have five or six puppies in a **litter**. Sometimes they have eight or nine. The newborns weigh as much as one or two lemons.

The pups are born with their eyes tightly shut. Their ears cannot hear yet. Their legs are too weak to hold up their bodies. Their tails are too weak to stand up. The newborns stay close to their mother. They feel warm and safe with her. They can eat and sleep all they want.

This cocker puppy is just one day old.

A lot happens in the puppies' first few weeks. Their eyes open up. Their ears begin to hear. Their tails stand up and start to wag. The pups get to know their brothers and sisters. They start to run around and play.

By the eighth week, the puppies' brains are ready to learn. This is a good time to start training the dogs. For the next few weeks, they will learn quickly. They are able to learn many **commands**. They can learn to sit, stay, come, beg, and roll over. They can also learn to fetch. Fetching is a great trick for puppies to learn. It teaches them to work with their owners.

Puppies must spend enough time with their mothers. If they do not, they might have problems later. Some get too shy. Others get mean or stubborn.

The cocker puppies in this litter are about six weeks old.

Cockers in Contests

Most owners just keep their cocker spaniels as pets. They like having them as friends. They enjoy walking, running, or hunting with them.

Many owners like to enter their cockers in **contests**. Some put their dogs in **obedience** contests. The dogs are graded on how well they follow commands.

This cocker is taking part in a dog show.

Other owners enter their cockers in **agility** contests. The dogs must run through an obstacle course. The obstacles include tunnels, see-saws, and ramps. The dogs must learn how to deal with the obstacles. They must go through, around, or over them. And then they must keep going. Speed counts!

Cockers often do well in agility contests. They are smart dogs. And they are full of energy. They are small, but they are speedy. They can run the courses quickly.

Some cockers work as **therapy** dogs. They visit people who are ill or could use a friend. They cheer people up with their sweet, gentle ways.

This cocker is jumping over bars in an agility contest.

Caring for a Cocker Spaniel

Cocker spaniels have been popular for years. People really love these cute dogs! But cockers' popularity has also caused problems. Too many people were raising and selling cockers. Some people raised and sold dogs that were not healthy. Because of this, many cockers now have health problems. People need to check on a dog's health before adopting it.

Healthy cockers like this one have shiny coats and bright eyes.

Even the healthiest cocker will have *some* problems. Owners should check their cockers' ears, coat, and skin often. The long ears pick up dirt and bugs easily. They should be checked every day and kept clean. The long coat should be brushed every day, too. This keeps it from getting tangled. Sometimes the coat needs to be clipped. Some cockers' skin gets dry, flaky, bumpy, or oily patches. A **veterinarian** can help with these skin problems.

Cocker spaniels need exercise, too. They should not stay indoors all the time. Healthy cockers can live to be about 15. And they can lead very happy lives!

Some cocker spaniels go to **grooming** shops. The groomers shampoo them. They cut their toenails. They brush their teeth. They even give the dogs breath spray!

A veterinarian is checking this cocker's ears for problems.

Glossary

agility (uh-JIH-luh-tee) Agility is being able to move quickly and easily. Cockers have great agility.

breeds (BREEDZ) Breeds are certain kinds of an animal. There are two breeds of cocker spaniel.

commands (kuh-MANDZ) Commands are orders to do certain things. Well-trained cockers follow commands.

contests (KON-tests) Contests are meets where people or animals try to win by being the best. Some people enter cocker spaniels in contests.

grooming (GROOM-ing) Grooming an animal is cleaning and brushing it. Cocker spaniels need lots of grooming.

litter (LIH-tur) A litter is a group of babies born to one animal. Cocker spaniel litters often have five or six puppies.

obedience (oh-BEE-dee-unts) Obedience is doing what someone says. Cocker spaniels can learn obedience.

obstacle (OB-stuh-kul) An obstacle is something that is in the way. Cockers do well on obstacle courses.

popular (PAH-pyuh-lur) When something is popular, it is liked by lots of people. Cocker spaniels are popular.

therapy (THAYR-uh-pee) Therapy is treatment for an illness or other problem. Visits from therapy dogs can make ill people feel better.

veterinarian (vet-rih-NAIR-ee-un) A veterinarian is a doctor who takes care of animals. Veterinarians are often called "vets" for short.

To Find Out More

Books to Read

American Kennel Club. *The Complete Dog Book for Kids.* New York: Howell Book House, 1996.

Beauchamp, Richard. *Cocker Spaniel: A Comprehensive Guide to Owning and Caring for Your Dog.* Allenhurst, NJ: Kennel Club Books, 2003.

Kane, Frank. *Cocker Spaniel.* Surrey, England: Ringpress Books, 1999.

Macaulay, Kelley, and Bobbie Kalman. *Cocker Spaniels.* New York: Crabtree Publishing, 2007.

Sucher, Jamie. *Cocker Spaniels.* Hauppauge, NY: Barron's Educational Series, 1999.

Places to Contact

American Kennel Club (AKC)
Headquarters
260 Madison Ave, New York, NY 10016
Telephone: 212-696-8200

On the Web

Visit our Web site for lots of links about cocker spaniels:

http://www.childsworld.com/links

Note to Parents, Teachers, and Librarians: We routinely check our Web links to make sure they're safe, active sites—so encourage your readers to check them out!

Index

About the Author

Susan H. Gray has a Master's degree in zoology. She has written more than 70 science and reference books for children. She loves to garden and play the piano. Susan lives in Cabot, Arkansas, with her husband Michael and many pets.